Butterfly Tales

*Motivating Stories of
Transition and Resilience
for Young Women*

2

Butterfly Tales

Written By: Tierica Berry

Butterfly Tales

Published by:
Affirmative Expression
PO Box 360856
Decatur, GA 30036

First edition copyright c 2013, Tierica Berry

Cover design by Michael "Panic" Haskin
PanicDoneCinap@gmail.com

Printed in the United States of America

ISBN: 978-0-615-86389-4

A Butterfly's Destiny...

Is *fed* as a **caterpillar**
Protected and **developed** in the **cocoon**
and **fulfilled** when she first spreads her
wings for the world to see the beautiful
butterfly she **ALWAYS** had potential to be...
-Tierica Berry

Table of Contents

Caterpillar Phase

The things that trouble your heart as a caterpillar will be a foggy memory once you've reached your butterfly Phase...

About this section...

This section consist of poems that tell the stories of various caterpillars trying to find their way. Some are written by teen ladies telling their own stories and some are written by me telling my story as well as the stories of others.

Some teens are occupied by issues at home, school, relationships, personal identity and self-image. This section calls attention to different stresses to let other young ladies know you are not alone when it comes to the feelings you are having and the issues you are experiencing.

It is my hope that you will find empowerment in knowing others have been where you are and survived to live another day. After reading this section please find yourself empowered to press on just like I did!

One Queen Per Castle

There is only one queen per castle I kept hearing her say
But it took me a long time to understand what she meant
I guess you could call me a daddy's girl in reference to the attention
given and time spent
And being the only daughter I didn't understand the battle I was born
into
There was this cycle of anger I had to get used to
Between my mother's hospital visits and mood swings she was kind of
hard to get close to
My brother, daddy and I would go visit her in the hospital but I might as
well had stayed at home
Because I would be fortunate to get as much as a, "Hello."
And this was my reality growing up with an underlying animosity
And again "There is only one queen per castle." I would hear her say
Daddy's work took him all over the world
Whenever daddy would leave
My mother would be nice to me
But one time when daddy was gone she was saying mean things
And being the daddy's girl I am I stood up for daddy
And my mother flipped on me!
She accused me of taking sides and stealing all her attention from daddy
We got into a big argument on the way home
But when we got to the house she was so quiet it gave me chills to my
bones
She sat in the living room and stared
Then I moved and she followed still staring
I could only imagine the things she was thinking about doing to me!
Then she said, "There is only one queen per castle!"
When daddy came home from his trip he heard about our fight
My mother had been painting me as the villain
He packed our things and said we were leaving
Just me and daddy going to stay with Uncle Ronnie
But I didn't understand why we had to leave if my mother was the one
always starting everything
Then he told me.
It was my fault. That I was the trouble maker.

I ruined the marriage between him and her
And I finally got it!
For the first time I knew what she meant.
With my older brother and daddy in the house she did not have to share her space
But when I was born, I stole her shine and as I got older she felt like she was being replaced
Her jealousy caused her to be ugly to me
And this was my reality growing up with an underlying animosity
And now I could barely get my own daddy to talk to me
"She ruined my marriage" is all I heard echoing
My mother had won.
She had successfully turned my daddy against me
And because we moved, she was once again the one and only queen.

Based on a true story
Stephanie
Age 16

I learned to be tough

I said I'm sorry
But it's not enough
'Cuz your love is too rough
And I'm not tough
I explain how I feel
And you tell me it's not real
I try to make you believe
While you think I'm trying to deceive
We have no trust
But it's a must
I forgave you
And became your slave
I did what I had to do
'Cuz I didn't know how to behave
Around this person who gave me one thing
But also nothing
She gave me life
While she was married to her wife
I wouldn't shed a tear
If I knew death was near
Knocking on her door
Preying on the poor
I was never good enough
But I learned to be tough

Based on a true story
Written by: Michela
Age: 17

HYPOTHETICALLY

Hypothetically speaking
What if I was mesmerized by your presence?
If I anticipated indulging in your essence?
What if I told you that I never hear what you say because your words are drowned out by your beauty?
I'm just asking.....you know.......**Hypothetically**
How about if I kissed you
just out of the blue
like I do when I dream about you?
Well you couldn't blame me
because lips like those are made for kissing
And people like you are made for missing
but remember **Hypothetically** I'm just asking!
Hypothetically if I got lost in your eyes
 don't send anyone for me
because the eye is the window to the soul
and that's exactly where I want to be.
I want to be consumed in everything that is you
oh......well.....you know, **Hypothetically**!
Hypothetically if I were wrapped up in your arms
 I would melt
Hypothetically if I were your woman
you would want for nothing else
and **Hypothetically** if I weren't so shy
 I would let you know that I am highly attracted to you!
I just thought I would let you know........ **Hypothetically**!

Secret

Excuse me for being frank but I have a confession
I am attracted to you.
You have a specific glow that appeals to me
but when I see you I am scared to admit this to you
I am scared because I am not sure what you might think
I try to give you hints and when you look away I may wink
Sometimes you catch me staring and sometimes I catch you too
Then I wonder if you are feeling the same way I do
Sometimes when we are close
I want you to wrap your hands around mine
and I would be lying if I told you
 that I have never imagined being your lady at some point in time
but this infatuation will never leave my book of poetry
because you and I could never exist in reality!

UnEvEn ExChAnGe

I still remember the first time that you crossed my path
I was shocked by your beauty and frozen in my tracks!
When your eyes connected with mine
I felt all of my insecurities begin to unwind
and I remember thinking,
"maybe he could be mine after a matter of time."
Your style of dress, the way you walked, and your confidence
compiled the perfect swagger
I think cupid got a promotion that day
because instead of being hit with an arrow
I was hit with a dagger!
And all of a sudden where you were
is where I wanted to be
But I had to play it cool until you shared the same emotions as
me.
Somewhere between us chillin' in public and chillin' in private
I somehow lost distinction between my reality and my fantisizin'
and I no longer knew whether you had come into my world and
shared the most intimate moments with me
or if once again my reality had been crossed with my fantasy.
Today I still want you as bad as the first time our eyes made that
connection
but I don't know how to approach you
and offer all of my affection
for fear of rejection
so I will just wait......for my own protection.
See, I have been saying that for a while and
the line is getting old
but the truth is
I'm bound by these things called words and
that's why the story remains untold.
What is love? Is it real?
Is it something we can see, hear, or feel?

Where can I find it? Where does it live?
If I can't see love is it possible to give?
Webster listed 24 definitions for the word 'Love'
and the best definition they could give was
"Strong affection for another arising out of kinship or personal ties"
Shortly after reading that definition
my closing statement began to arise.
The dictionary alone could do no justice
for my emotions toward you
because I have a crush on you
because I long for you
and if beginner's love is real then baby I got that too!
When I see you I undress your soul with my eyes
but every time you pass me by
a small girl deep inside of my heart cries
And my emotion radar detects light showers
with a chance of harsh rain
I want you to know that I'm talking to you
so I almost want to say your name
but I have to get over you
because this pursuit is causing me too much pain
If something were to happen in which I lost my memory
and had not an ounce of knowledge in my brain
I may not know that roses are red
and I may not be sure if violets are blue
but I will always know that love is what I feel when I am with you!

Glass Box

Have you ever prayed for something?
Not like for a good day or oh Lord please let these shoes be on sale
I mean *REALLY* prayed for something
or, have you ever thought like this:
If this person had that person's personality, and this person's chivalry,
that person's eyes, and that person's swag, and that person's
generosity, and this person's affection, and this person's love, and that
person's ability to listen, and that person's class, and this person's
height, and that person's good looks THEY WOULD BE PERFECT!!!!
Now imagine if all these things plus some
were to manifest in one person
and this one person came into your life and
extinguished your desire for anyone else
past, present and future
After life crossed our paths
we began spending a lot of time together and
fell for each other like two school kids
I wanted him to be mine and he wanted me to be his
But circumstances and situations
kept us from moving to the next level
My emotions aren't like lights
I can't just switch them on and off at the drop of a dime
He can't expect me to be ok with him saying,
"we need to take some time."
When I see him I can tell he struggles with this too
but he is a man so I don't think he struggles with it like I do
I want him to know the entirety of how I feel
but I have no clue where to start.
I fumble for the words but stumble upon tears instead
Have you ever cried from the bottom of your heart?
I mean crying until no more sounds will come out
Curled up in the middle of the floor unable to control your muscles like,
"God, what is this about?"
Crying can be interpreted as a sign of weakness
So, before I leave the house every morning
I plaster a smile on my face

and put the pieces of my broken heart in my purse
I hold my head high and carry my purse with care
because only God knows how much it hurts
I have held my dream in these very arms
only for it to be pried from these same arms
and placed in this glass box for my torment
It's bad enough to know everything you've dreamed of exists on this earth and you can't have it
but to still have to see it everyday
is a bit much for the toughest of hearts
Here I sit quiet enough to hear my tears drop
face pressed against his glass box
really praying for a sign
Lord if it is your will that I wait patiently
until it is our time to be one in the sight of God
So be it! Or would you call me to move on and mark this angel as just another page in my poetry book?
How do I know when enough is enough?
How do I know when our well has finally dried up?
Or when it is time to jump back into the dating game?
Would it not be fair to him
since another man is running through my brain?
Will I end up making subconscious comparatives
observing how, mmm, this is different, oooh but this is the same!
Then in the middle of writing this poem it hit me!
If this man is truly mine
we will be together when I get myself together
If my heart is designated for another
he will blow my mind in ways I am currently unable to fathom
So until that appointed moment in time I will diligently prepare myself
for my king but more importantly for me
If the time I spent with my dream is worth nothing else
it has raised my bar
to let me know I am worth much more than I have been receiving.

Not Any Ordinary Evening

The room is pitch black as far as I can see
and at this moment I am sulking in my misery
The walls are closing in
I'm beginning to feel sick
It seems I'll never win
so there's no need to kick
I'm on my back in the bed
little light is peering under the door
Last I checked I had two legs
tonight it seems as if I have four
Tears began to flow like water from Niagara Falls
but no sounds are coming out none at all
I close my eyes praying I will wake up from this nightmare
I didn't do anything to deserve this
It just isn't fair!
I've finally come to the realization this is all real
and in actuality there is another body on top of me.

Coulda, Shoulda, Woulda...

I coulda told him no
I shoulda turned to go
I woulda had more pride to show
I coulda told the truth
I shoulda resisted his juice
I woulda had better things to do
I coulda called the cops
I shoulda made him stop
I woulda made the page on top
I coulda left faster
I shoulda left right after
I woulda pleased the master
I coulda grabbed the gun
I shoulda told someone
I woulda had this whole thing done
I coulda stopped our relations
I shoulda cut conversation
I woulda had him out of the equation
There are things I did and things I didn't
But no matter what, in stone, history is written
All of this I could have been prevented
I shoulda, I coulda, I woulda,
...but I didn't!

Daddies Kiss Your Daughters

The key to finding what you need
is to know what it looks like
How can a girl know what to expect of a man
if she doesn't even know she is entitled to expectations
Fathers are supposed to show their daughters how she is supposed to
be treated by living up to her mother's expectations
Daddies have to touch their daughters
kiss them and hug them
so they know how a touch feels that is inspired by only love
If not they will long for the touch of a man
but will mistake lustful groping
for a genuinely affectionate touch
Being a daddy is more than just sending money
because contrary what society wants you to think
money ain't everything
Money can't teach you how to ride a bike
Money can't money can't tap that behind
to keep you in line
Money can't make you laugh when you are down
Money can't protect you from the predators lurking around
Money can't give your date 3rd degree before it sees you off to prom
Nor can it be sitting on the couch waiting for you to get home
Money can't walk you down the aisle
on your wedding day
Money can't hold back tears
before it gives you away
only a daddy can...
Daddies kiss your daughters!
The state of our society depends on you
If one kiss could keep one girl off the stripper pole
if one kiss could keep another girl off the pipe
if one kiss could keep that girl's legs closed
if one kiss could bring my little sister home every night
would you do it?
Would you kiss her and tell her you really missed her

Would you tell her you are sorry you didn't give her the affection that
was due to her
We didn't ask to be here
your actions blessed you with beautiful daughters
Now do what you have to do so the daughters in the world
grow into beautiful women
Daddies your daughters really need you!
Look at her, she is crying on the inside
can't you see it in her eyes?!
Take some time and really pry
to see what is wrong with your daughter
Think really hard
is there anything else you could have taught her?
Is there anything else you could have told her
to protect her from this already difficult life that lay ahead of her...?

Internal Bleeding

My little girl has something to say.
I can no longer cover her mouth with caution tape
Nor can I continue to filter what she has to say
I knew there was only so long
I could hide her behind this shelled exterior
before the world would finally hear from her
So many words
so much pain I have been harboring inside
it was like swallowing marbles assuming I would eventually be ok
if I just let it ride...
At fourteen I was molested
but I felt like I shared the blame
He made me feel like a big girl
but it was all a part of his sick game
I always heard horrific rape stories
that made mine sound so minuet.
I thought if I was looking for some sympathy
I would be told I was being dramatic
and to look at how bad all these other kids had it.
So I put a few pages in my poetry book and moved on
In my mind this was me facing my problems head on.
For me it was like letting a lion taste blood
I was looking for something and didn't know what it was
I now know this caused me to be promiscuous
thinking I would somehow benefit from giving it up.
I didn't have those core values properly instilled in me
I didn't grasp the true value and significance of the treasures God
had given me!
Lacking the knowledge on how to be a lady
I surely didn't know how to treat a man!
So I did what I thought I should do
and that was find the man who offered the most security
love him as hard as I could possibly love.

and the true man, that was really meant for me
would never leave...
This quest was doomed from the start
and it turned me into a monster
all the while my little girl inside was absorbing the hurt
I had friends of the family, teachers, and strangers
trying to have their way
despite the fact they were fully aware of my age!
Although I led on like everything was ok
my wound had not healed all the way
like when you stub your pinky
and before it can heal you stub it again
A lot of women live their lives like this until they die
they die bitter old women and the world wonders why
Well it's because when they were little girls
some grown ass man robbed them of their innocence
causing them to grow up too fast
So think about that the next time you want to call a little girl fast!
Black women have a reputation of being strong women
and that's what these little girls are trying to be
so they mend their own wounds which never heal
they just remain buried
Searching for something to ease this pain that ailed me
I just wanted someone to need me...
Sometimes when I was hurt or angry
I could lay as still as my muscles would allow
and it was like I could feel myself or something inside of me
kicking, breaking things, and screaming
fist and jaw clenched tear ducts on overload
back then I didn't understand what it was
but now I know...
it was my little girl.
After my most recent break up, once again I was taunted
she was so close to getting what she always wanted
she was looking for something all these years

she needed someone to protect her
someone constant.
someone to give her unconditional and uninhibited love and
attention
So there you have it
this is not a character I created
this is not Defyne
this is not even Tierica Berry.
This is as naked as my soul can get
I am that little girl
encouraging that little girl or boy inside of you
to open up and stop the internal bleeding
so your wounds can heal...

Cocoon Phase

This will probably be the most critical phase in your metamorphosis. Be still and be alert. The universe will give you clues to help you transition into your butterfly phase. Your cocoon is designed to protect you during this transition. Be cautious of who and what you all to influence you during this time...

About this section...

This section is about the phase in your life when you realize there is something greater in store for you. Its when you start to finally listen to that inner voice that has been trying to guide you this whole time!

This phase is very important because sometimes we may allow people in our cocoon that mean us no good and they will cripple our growth and stunt our potential!

In this section you will find some poems written from that inner voice and you will find some poems that challenge the voice that means us no good.

Listen...

Rosa Mae

This particular dream took me back to January 28, 2010
but the sun shinned brighter than I remember
and it was warmer than it was back then
My subconscious anxiety about walking thru the graveyard
had dissipated
It was as if my fear had been replaced with empowerment
from the unfulfilled dreams
of the souls resting under my feet
I followed the music to the tent, same location
only the tent was purple this time
and under it sat my beautiful Aunt Rose
She was playing her piano
and she looked astonishing in her white robe
She lifted her head and smiled at me
Her make-up was flawless
like it was applied with angel wings
She told me to take a seat next to her
but she never stopped playing
the most beautiful music I never heard
I said, "Aunt Rose I miss you."
she said, "Baby I never left, I just transferred into a different
energy,
A positive energy for you and whoever else is listening
It broke my heart to see those things happened with the family
after I left my physical body
and you would think after knocking over that tree
they would at least pretend
they wanted to do the right thing
but that's neither here nor there.
I want to tell you, Tierica
to never give up on your dreams
I know sometimes you fear rejection and failure
but to your core, you are a fighter with a gift of insight

don't let the people of this world
tell you what you can't do
make sure the people that would love to see you fall
watch you go harder and further
than they ever dreamed to
stay close to your family but don't let them interfere
or distract you from your goals and the journey of getting there
you can't change the world
but you have the power to touch some hearts
you will do great things in your future and
your poetry is where it starts
Now, wake up my little angel and take the world by storm
like you were destined to do since the day you were born..."

Confession

He first came to me in a dream
As I slept subconsciously he convinced me to join his team
When I awoke he was just as beautiful as I'd dreamed
and I followed his alluring trail wherever he went
He spoke to me in unfamiliar tongues
with a consistent rhythm that made me addicted to his songs
He took me on highs my mind could never fathom
He followed me through lows when tears were the outcome
He was something no one else had ever been to me
He became more than a friend to me
Since day one he has had me intoxicated
and wanting to sing his praises to everyone
The epitome of him is indescribable by words
Who knew he could make me sing like a bird?
I like for us to be out on display
but I love our intimate moments alone
This infatuation is far too deep to keep between just him and me
From this moment on I am telling everyone, I am in love with POETRY....

Reality Bitters the Sweet

Baby girl, enjoy playing with your
tea cups and baby dolls
and the time when your biggest concern is if mommy is going to make
you wear those not so pretty overalls
when a long day is extra laps in P.E.
followed by double chores when you get home
and you against the world is mommy not letting you stay up past eight
on the phone
and when heart ache is
little Johnny asking someone else to the dance
when the two of you are clearly a couple
since last week when you let him hold your hand
when the hardest decision you had to face today was
who will wear the part of your best friends' necklace that says 'Best'
and winding down from your day
is a nap on daddy's chest
It may seem like a lot now
but treasure these simplicities like they are gold
because you would probably trade the world to have it back once you
get old
Play times will be harder to come by
when you are down to your last dime
and I bet those overalls won't even cross your mind
when your biggest concern is trying to pay all these bills on time
and a long day is working two jobs to take care of yourself and
the ones you love
then coming home to cook, clean, and take a quick nap before you have
to wake up and repeat all of the above
You against the world will be
politicians raising the taxes for middle class
and your boss trying to get you fired over some petty drama that caused
your personalities to clash
and now, heart ache is giving the man you love your everything
only to realize you are not the type he would ever give a ring
You will treasure the good ole days
when hardest decision you had to face today

was to ignore your growling stomach
or overdraft your account at the bank
So take this word from the wise
Enjoy your innocence while you are still sweet as pie
because reality is a cold hearted witch
that will make you cry
I could tell you every day to be sweet
and don't let anyone or anything change you
but deep down I know the inevitable truth
and pretty soon you will too
REALITY BITTERS THE SWEET...

Unlike a Clock I am Inconsistent

Tick. Tock. Tick. Tock.
This is what I hear as I watch the clock.
Consistently fulfilling its sole purpose in life
keeping time
And as I watch the clock I can't help but think of what I am losing,
time
As the second hand whirls around,
landing on each and every number
I contemplate my life and the everyday stresses I am under
Thousands of small dilemmas add to big stress.
And the faster the issues run through my mind
the harder they are to express.
What do I do when someone from the outside wants in?
How can I make them relate, when I don't know where to begin?
Before I can utter one sentence three more appear
then I get frustrated because what I am saying
is not what I want them to hear
So I shut down, try to regroup and organize my words
and by the time I finish thinking
my mind has convinced me the whole situation was absurd
So my mouth says, "Never mind, nothing is wrong."
and my soul is aching from continuously holding my tongue
but I ease my soul with the rule of discretional speaking
and yet again I am left wondering
What is my sole purpose in life?
Is it to just be a daughter, or one day be a wife,
to motivate my friends, or to birth new life?
Am I supposed to live for me?
Or am I supposed to live so that everyone around me is happy?
If I decided not to complete my task what would become of me?
What if the clock decided to stop ticking?
It doesn't work like that, it's not the way of the world!

A baby boy will not come out of the womb screaming he wanted
to be a girl!
Everyone is put here for a reason to serve a specific purpose.
But the soul searching is driving me insane.
I'm going to let you in on a secret that sometimes crosses my
brain
I often think about all of the agony we tolerate every day
and wonder why?
Wouldn't it be easier to just pass on to the next life?
I know you probably think I am crazy
But think about it wouldn't it be easier
than being restricted to your body
the mobile prison that is the source of your pain?
But where's the glory in taking the easy way out?
So I guess I have to stay here, suck it up, and stick it out.
Maybe one day I will know exactly why I am here
Then I will look back at this poem, then look at the clock
and I am willing to bet I will still hear that constant
Tick. Tock.

Choices

I sit here with a feeling of loneliness
wondering what will happen next
Staring into the dark
for answers that are simple and direct
but years and years of staring into the dark
for answers that are bright
can be tiring and strenuous on the eyes
if you do it night after night
So I give my eyes a rest an put my ears to work
I close my eyes and listen to the blaring sounds of silence
until my ears begin to hurt
So I listen to my gut, my instinct
you know, women's intuition
but after listening to that for a while
I realized it didn't grant the answer I'd been wishin'
So I go against my soul
and do what my mind thinks is right
and I find myself right back in the cold and loneliness of the night
But this time there were doors, four of them
Then a strong voice said, "you must pick a door
Just one of them. Through this door you must jump, this is the
jump of life and it can be made only once"
So I looked them over carefully
giving them each plenty of thought
Doors 2-4 had plenty of lights
but door number 1 was dark
and kind of faded into the night
Three is my favorite number
so I gambled with my chance
I gripped the door knob turned it and did a happy dance
through the door I jumped with my eyes shut tight
and I listened until I heard a song that fancied my delight
to my surprise when I opened my eyes I was in paradise

but all the while I didn't realize
I was slipping dipper into my fate
just happy to be where I was
not realizing it was all slipping away from my face
Then it got a little dark and grew a little colder
when I felt a warm hand grasp my shoulder
"What have I done why am I here" I asked the mystery man
The same strong voice leaped from the dark
"It's all part of God's master plan.
What shines in the beginning is failure later on
But work hard for what you want and you can't go wrong!"
A question still lurked in my mind, "Can I try again?"
Then I remembered what was stated before I even began.
"This is the jump of life it will be made only once..."
and because I went after the wrong thing I feel like a dunce.
Just remember the jump determines your fate
and I'm just trying to let you know before it's too late.

Limitations of the Mind

I can't, impossible, and unattainable
Are only a few verbal limitations set by the mind
just mental boundaries to stop the advancement of mankind
People are taught to be miserable
they become poor, sick beggars by tradition
and parents pass it to subsequent generations
then moan and groan about their conditions
But we are quick to snap an excuse
when something threatens our helplessness
I was once told, excuses are tools of the incompetent
used to build monuments of nothing
In the Bible it says God is strength,
It also says that the Spirit of the Lord is in you.
so if these things hold true
wouldn't that mean that the sky is the limit for you too?
Sitting around trying to sell yourself a story
on why you can't get ahead
waking up day after day going to a job you dread
more scared to succeed than you are to fail
living in limbo creating your own living hell
I don't know about you
but I can do all things
through Christ who strengthens me
The fear of pain shouldn't be a factor for anybody
Pain is only weakness leaving the body
even if you've never been to college
you should always strive to further your knowledge
because if you only know what you've always known
you will only be who you've always been.

How Dare You

Ok God I was walking along minding my own business
Things were going fine
until out of nowhere you pushed me
I fell to the ground, scraped my elbow,
I even bruised my knee
And for what?!
Were you trying to see if I could still fee?
Well did you get your answer
because these tears are real!
Or was it just because you are Almighty God and you can?
And I can't do anything about it
because I am only a man
not even a man but a woman.
I tell you what I am going to get up from this sidewalk
and brush myself off
I've come too far to go down like that I ain't soft!
Before I could get off the ground
A weight came over me like it weighed 500 pounds
And as clear as day I heard my Lord speak to me
He said,
"You have some nerve letting such objections come from your face
Every time you get up whether it is from the ground our from your bed
its by my grace
You are my child!
I know how many hairs are on your head
so of course I know you 'aint soft'
but it's only because I made you that way
and how dare you belittle your womanhood
I didn't design you to be less than a man, but his equal
However, neither man nor woman is any match for me
for I am supernatural
But everyday what I try to get you to see is
I am not the enemy
When you were walking along minding 'your own business'
I pushed you down onto the sidewalk
Yes you scraped your elbow and bruised your knee

but that pain was nothing like the pain that would have been delivered
from that SUV
I pushed you to protect you
but tears of temporary pain and emotion blurred your vision as the SUV
sped past
So next time try not to think with emotions
and jump to conclusions so fast!"
And by the Grace of God I got up from that sidewalk
With a scrape and a bruise to remind me of his mercy
So the next time God pushes you praise him anyway
Because you never know,
 there could have been a bus coming your way...

Self Destruction

Left...

                          Right...

Left...

                          Right...

My staggering footsteps carry me
only God knows where
like the natives of this land
sobbing and heaving leaving a trail of tears
Through tear filled eyes I see cloudy images of people being held
prisoner to their own flesh
My ears have zoned out like I am in a tunnel
and all I hear are my short inconsistent breaths
my heart is heavy and my mind is constantly plagued with
obligations to which I need to tend
it's nobody's fault but my own
but I feel like I've reached wits end
GOD IM TIRED!
I'm tired of the decisions I've been making
so sick of being in this situation
I constantly wreck my brain for a quick solution
but to no avail
So my staggering footsteps carry me toward the stairwell
Left...

                          Right...

Left...

                          Right...

My legs grow tired as I climb flight after flight
finally reaching the roof top I prepare myself mentally to be set
free from this prison that is me

                          Right...

Left...

I approach the ledge and my hands begin to shake
Spreading my arms

I surrender myself to my fate my footsteps went-
Left...
                    Right...
Left...
                    Right over the side of the wall
Gravity was my accomplice in this self destruction
increasing my speed during this ultimate free fall
Memories fill my head and stream from my tear ducts
Eyes wide shut...
          Jaw clenching...
                    Teeth grinding...
                              Preparing for impact...
No sense in screaming this was not a mistake
No I would not take it back
A woman's scream pierces my ears milliseconds before I connect
with the pavement below
I slowly stand up while brushing myself off and press through the
crowd of nosey onlookers
Glancing over my shoulder I see EMS and police
Mission Accomplished!
From here on out I vow to stay away from anything that
contributed to the self destruction of the OLD me.

Mirrors Never Lie

Mirror, mirror on the wall
all this stress and pain tell me who's responsible for it all
(...and the mirror replied)
"How long do you expect to go on like this before you realize running
from me will never be the answer?
You've been constantly running for all these years and as you can see
I'm still here
through all the mess you've allowed yourself to get into at the end of
the day I'm the one you have to answer to
In the past your insecurity has caused you to overcompensate and look
for acceptance in all the wrong places
landing you in evil men's laps
and smiling in trifling girls' faces
Your ignorance and desire to be accepted
has made you call these posers friends
Why can't you catch on to this pattern
it keeps happening again and again!
Every time these men, boys, predators abuse your kindness, and invade
your promise land, treasure place, your temple they vanish from your
life
and after your "girlfriends" feel as if you are no longer willing to let
them use you for their personal gain they are gone
And guess who? It's me again!
Just you and I trying to stay afloat in your tears
and figure out once again how in the world you got here.
But the part that always gets me is you go out and do it again!
When will you learn you have to do something different for this cycle to
end!
Running is not going to help you better yourself
So take off your running shoes, sit down, and try something else
First you have to be ok with being alone
you may surround yourself with people for company
but standing in the middle of Time Square you can still be alone!
Please realize you can point the blame all you want to
but people have only done
what you have allowed them to do!

Stand strong for what you believe
Stand up for whom and what you love
Put your feelings before others
because trust me everyone else does
No more crying over people who wouldn't shed a tear for you
That's tears in a bucket
and you can miss me with that too
No more running from person to person
fueling your co-dependence
No more contemplations of self-inflicted pain
No more fleeing at the first sign of rain
No more seeking temporary satisfaction
No more giving it up easily in hopes of a mutual attraction
No more "needing to be needed"
You need yourself and that's all the needing you need!
From now on if anybody or anything comes in the way of you getting
where you need and want to be
keep it moving!
Stay true to God and stay true to yourself
Before you move on with your day I need you to promise me this...
'Promise me you will strive to be the classy, elegant, respectable, smart,
trusted, righteous, beautiful woman you have always wanted to be,
promise to never stop striving and never take a break. Strive until you
achieve and once you've achieved then you work on over achieving. Be
an inspiration, a role model for generations to come. Use your past
mistakes as stepping stools as well as teaching tools. Make that promise
to me, the woman in the mirror, every morning and don't break it
because remember I will know!'
Oh yeah! And to answer your initial question,
"who's to blame for it all?" --"You are!"

I'm Here for You

Think lines sink deep
into skin the color of chocolate. Semi-sweet.
grays in his beard just enough to count
each gray symbolic of another victory against being down and out
Laugh lines lie just under his beard
from every time he laughed in the face of failure
every time he overcame adversity and remained so pure
pure but not naïve makes this man a treasure for sure
Shoulders broad enough to bear the burdens of the ones he loves
Arms long and large for rejuvenating hugs
with a massive chest capable of absorbing the most painful of tears
Hands big and strong enough to build up a community
yet gentle enough to console and wipe a tear from your cheek
This man is a man from the crown of his head
to the sole of his feet
but if you look deep into his brown eyes
you may catch a glimpse of the pain he tries to hide
this pain not hidden with intent to deceive
but protect his loved ones from being burdened
by burdens they don't need
I can only hope when he decides to put down his burdens
and he needs someone to rub his back
or when he has given one too many hugs
and needs someone to hug him back
after all the communities are built
but the to-do list still stands ten feet tall
or when staying strong for everyone else
leaves just enough strength for one phone call
I hope that phone call is to me
and I can only wish that I can be everything to him
that he has been to me
If some kind of way I could ease his brain
If there is any possible way to alleviate his pain
and make everything he deems a problem go away
I would do it in a heartbeat!
I would press his face into my bosom where tears disappear

hold him in my arms and tell him, "You are safe here, because these arms belong to the one who loves you!"

Butterfly Phase

*With a clearer understanding of who you
are you will find your wings, with your new
found confidence you will soar to heights
never imagined, and the world will smile...*

About this section...

This section might be my favorite section because it never ends. In this section poetry comes from a place of confidence. In this phase of your life you will feel a sense of awareness, happiness, and belonging.

I am still writing this chapter of my life and although you will always have days where you may feel like a caterpillar or like you are back in your cocoon, the goal is to feel generate more and more Butterfly Tales...

Enjoy...

Take Me as I Am

If you can't accept me on my bad days
You don't deserve me on my good days!
To all of you that have ever made me feel I was
too black
too fat
too short
too loud
too clumsy
too weak
too emotional
too soft spoken
too country
too proper
and those of you who said
my breasts are too big
my butt is too big
my gut is too big
and those of you who think
my natural hair is not long enough
or I'm not pretty enough
not skinny enough
I'm not dainty enough
or not polished enough
those of you who don't like my laugh
or disagree with the fun times I've had
to those of you who judge me for the mistakes I made and think my
spirit needs to be tamed
you almost had me!
Trying to force your opinions on me!
I used to be so naïve
trying to fit into a box
based on your opinion of who you thought I should be.
What I didn't know was, the box never existed
and even if it did, a spirit like mine would never fit in it.
If you need some ideas on where to put that imaginary box I can think
of a few places you could stick it!

If I only knew then, what I know now
there's no telling where I would be
So with my new confidence
and feeling comfortable with me
I will hold my head high and
tell you I am just fine in this skin of mine
People are going think what they think
and say what they say
but I am a beautiful person EVERYDAY!
and if you don't like it you can kick rocks or
Just take me as I am...

My New Pumps

Many times before I have said I was going to do better and
I was going to change
The difference is this time I didn't plan a change
I didn't try to compare my life to the role models of America
I didn't buy a book with a 12 step program on
'How to be a better Tierica'
I just woke up
I woke up and said this is not who I am
I am a lady so that's how I should start behaving.
I have had so many people feed into my life to help shape me into
the woman I should be
but no one knows what woman I should be
better than me
Then I realized what I was doing wrong
I was starting with the outside
how other people saw me
No matter how dainty and classy
I presented myself to be
people would always see straight through the windows
to the ugly side in me
the part that was unsettled and unhappy
the little girl in me that was seeking something she should have
gotten from her mommy and daddy
Don't get me wrong I love my parents with all my heart
but after all these years
I know there was something missing in my heart
and as a result I searched the world for that missing part
Now you compare that to digging for diamonds!
People in my circle would give me diamonds
I just had a hard time separating the diamond
from the muck
but I thought I had it all figured out
because I was following a rubric

some seemingly successful woman laid out
This is equivalent to taking someone else's prescribed medication
without seeing the doctor for yourself
I'm not blaming anyone for my mistakes
or for the bad decisions I have made
I place that blame 100% on myself
I do not possess the pen to rewrite history
nor do I have a blanket large enough to keep my mistakes
mysteries
but there comes a time in every girl's life
where she is given an opportunity evolve into a woman
It's up to that girl if she will strive or not even try
Well finally my decision has been made
I'm trading in my penny loafers for pumps
my bonbon lip balm for MAC lipstick
and I'm not looking back!
I am fully aware there are people who will try and judge me for
who I used to be
I wish I had a thousand lives to give the people that have nothing
better to do than ruin mine
but wishes to change the past will remain wishes
until the end of time
I do, however, suggest you check your own closet before you
come digging through mine!
I am so much smarter than the girl I used to be
and I want to thank you all especially the haters for challenging
the woman in me

I'SE A WOMAN NAH!!!

My World My Rules
I refuse to live in a world where I am fed who I am supposed to be thru TV
I live in my own world where I can express myself creatively
In my world I am the sole guardian of my own psyche warding off any and all negativity
That energy you feel when I come around is the universe's positive energy flowing directly through me
Go ahead and soak up what you can because my cup runeth over
People wonder why they can't quite get a hold on me
That's because I am going places I am following my own destiny
I just pray God guides my footsteps and continues to enlarge my territory
I pray that God's light shines through me
and I can be a prime example of what living life to the fullest is supposed to be
I refuse to live in fear
Fear is a lack of faith in God
Most people have more faith in their GPS than they have in their own creator
A wise young man once broke this down for me in an excellent analogy
He said I follow directions from a tracking system in the sky without hesitation
Despite the fact that from my position I cannot see my destination
But God has given us turn by turn directions to life but you are still seeking further explanation
Technology is successfully turning us into a lost generation
I am determined to press on
I will experience every ounce of joy until my time has expired here
I will continue to break generational curses and broaden horizons
I will teach the ones around me that young is a state of mind
Laughter is the best medicine
And true friendship lasts beyond the end of time
Your stigmas and stipulations will not hold me back
In your world under your rules reaching for the stars may be the best you can do
but I won't just reach for the stars I will look down from the universe because this is my world, my rules!

Futuristic girl

With skin a hue of blue
more soothing than the deep blue sea
and fire red hair
to show the feisty side in me
I am a walking contradiction
A perfect imperfection
Lost in my own world on purpose
with no hopes of being found
No need for mirrors, make up or even clothes
to define my beauty
I don't need superficial associates around for company
I'm fine here all alone
entertaining myself with the different dimensions of me
To you, I am so far from everything
but to me I am surrounded with everything I need
Beyond Earth's atmosphere for the first time
I have finally found true peace
Not bound by the laws that govern your land

I   am   finally   free

Just as a real man does not have to declare he is a man
you can just look at me know
you have never seen anything like me
not in your city, not even in your world
because I'm just a futuristic girl!

Beautiful

In the moments when the moon
shares the sky with the sun
golden rays reach from behind the clouds
that hide the sun
This beauty feels as though it were made just for me
but I know I'm not the only one
In the still of the night
when the moon is the brightest source of light
if I were the only one gazing it just wouldn't be right!
More times than not we get caught up
with the hustle and bustle of life
and forget to enjoy the beautiful slices of the pie
we are often told to take the good with the bad
but it's better to move past your troubles
and enjoy what good is left while you still can.
This is the way to maximize joy in its purest form
What good is a rainbow
if you're still thinking about the storm?!

Your
Metamorphosis

Now it is your time to share your metamorphosis process...

Write about Your Caterpillar Phase

During this phase of your life the things that affect you the most may be very insignificant to you when you are flying through your Butterfly phase. However it is important to honor your feelings and a great idea to write them down so you can see how far you have come...
We all make mistakes in every phase but in your caterpillar phase you learn valuable mistakes that help shape your morals and ways of thinking. Write about some mistakes you made that changed your way of thinking or specific thoughts you had.

_____

_____

_____

_____

_____

_____

_____

_____

_____

_____

_____

_____

_____

_____

_____

_____

_____

_____

_____

_____

_____

_____

_____

_____

_____

Write about your Cocoon Phase

It is important to know when you are mentally ready to enter your Cocoon Phase. This requires a certain level of maturity. During this time you are very impressionable and you have to be careful who you allow to influence you. The cocoon will serve as your shield from unnecessary nonsense. Take this time to be still and you can determine who and what influences the type of butterfly you will become. Write about some times you were very still and answers seemed to come to you almost out of nowhere.

_____

_____

_____

_____

_____

_____

_____

_____

_____

_____

_____

_____

_____

_____

_____

_____

_____

_____

_____

_____

_____

_____

_____

_____

Write about your Butterfly Phase

This is section is very special and unique because if you are flying like you were destined to fly this section will never be complete! I am still writing my Butterfly section and soon you will know exactly what I mean! During this phase of your metamorphosis you will have a clearer understanding of who you are and what you really like. Why don't you start with some poems or short stories about who you are?

_____

_____

_____

_____

_____

_____

_____

_____

_____

_____

_____

_____

_____

_____

_____

_____

_____

_____

_____

_____

_____

_____

_____

_____

Tierica has EMPOWERING and EDUCATIONAL workshops and presentations for WOMEN and YOUTH. To obtain more information or if you are interested in having Tierica come to SPEAK for your organization please use one of the following means of contact below

Tierica opens GEARUP Day @ Wichita State University

Email:
AffirmativeExpression@gmail.com
Phone:
678.216.7387
Or visit:
AffirmativeExpression.Com

MANY THANKS FROM THE POET

I would first like to give thanks to God for not only blessing me with this talent to put my feelings and observations into words that people can feel and understand but also for giving me the courage to share my talent with the world

I would like to thank Hotep and Hustle University for providing the insight and nudge I needed to make my work more marketable and providing the lane I needed to accomplish my goal!

Shout out Panic for creating such an awesome cover! Thanks for always coming through on the graphics! Also Fray wall for the photo shoot capturing my images and making me look graceful! LOL!
I would also like to thank my four loving parents, Angela, Arthur, Robert, and Salina that have always supported me in my creativity.
Most importantly I want to thank YOU for taking the time to read my innermost thoughts and I pray you have enjoyed every piece and walk away satisfied.

Thank you,
With all the love in my heart,
Tierica Berry

As a token of my appreciation I want to give you a sneak preview to my next project titled:

Stained Glass

"Broken has never been so beautiful..."

Stained Glass

The definition of broken
Reduced to fragments, fragmented, not working properly
I have been broken
Some situations were out of my control. Some of my brokenness was
self-induced
Either way, I have been broken, fragmented, reduced to fragments
This a fact not an excuse

For years I have tried to pull my pieces together and get ahold of me
Asking God to reveal what all this cracks and fragments really mean
I've been thru the fire with these stains and scars
So no matter how much I tried aint no washing that off
While trying to assemble these fragments in the way I think they should
go
And grow my life in the way I think it should grow
I caught a glimpse of this beautiful stained glass window
And I tried to imagine how much artistic skill is required to create such a
masterpiece
And I wondered what kind of masterpiece could be created if I allowed
God to do the same with me
Could I be like this stained glass window and adopt all of its properties?
Because each fragment of glass is carefully arranged in a unique pattern
That is identity
These patterns are then supported by a rigid frame
That's strength
Each window must then fit snugly into the space for which it was made
That is purpose
And when that window is ready it has to hold its own weight and
weather the storm
That is endurance
It must maintain its level of beauty and elegance without being
conformed
And that is resilience

Resilience, endurance, purpose, strength, and identity
With a clearer understanding of these properties I am able to get a clear
understanding of me

Glass in its pure state is unscathed, whole, and transparent
But I have been stained. Scared and tainted

Yes I am broken and yes I have been stained
But you will never see a stained brokenness more beautiful than this
I stand tall and proud for all the world to behold
This unique imperfection that is my stained glass window
We are taught to ignore and bury our cracks
No! Rise up from your brokenness and embrace that!
Each stain allows the world to see God from a different light
And each crack tells a different story
When you truly embrace your cracks and stains as your divine identity
you too will be the most beautiful stained glass the world has ever seen

27607151R00060

Made in the USA
Charleston, SC
15 March 2014